Between Two Worlds

Américo Paredes

Arte Publico Press
Houston
Texas
1991

This volume is made possible by a grant from the National Endowment for the Arts, a federal agency.

Arte Publico Press
University of Houston
Houston, Texas 77204-2090

Paredes, Américo.
Between Two Worlds / Américo Paredes.
    p. cm.
English and Spanish.
ISBN 1-55885-022-8
1. Mexican Americans—Poetry.   I. Title.
PS3531.A525B48 1990
811'.54–dc20   90-38832
                                                                    CIP

The paper used in this publication meets the minimum requirements of the American National Standard for Permanence of Paper for Printed Library Materials Z39.48-1984. ∞

Wandering between two worlds, one dead,
The other powerless to be born . . .

—Matthew Arnold

Contents

From *Cantos a Carolina* (1934 – 1946)

Prologue

On September 3, 1960, I attained the age of forty-five and what I judged was a mature and stable state of mind; so I decided it was time to destroy the fruits of my labors in what, with a good deal of poetic license, might be called poetry. These had been piling up in varied envelopes and manila folders for more than thirty years. Some of them, done in Spanish mostly, had already been set loose upon the world in various publications. *Palo dado ni Dios lo quita.* But most of them were at hand in yellowing pieces of paper of all shapes and sizes. In the ensuing months I did destroy a goodly number of them, those that were so painfully bad I could not bear to look at them twice. But I never got around to consigning all of them to the flames. For one thing, I was convinced that a dozen or so were worth saving, though I never could decide which dozen or so they might be. For another, all the survivors had personal value for me, whatever their lack of literary merit. So I put off the holocaust until I too should be closer to cremation. In the years that followed I even added a few more to the pile.

My sixty-fifth birthday should have been a good date for the burning, but important events had taken place since 1960. The dream of my young and isolated years had been made a reality by a new generation. A young *mejicano* intelligentsia had coalesced into a Movimiento Chicano, and along with it a Chicano literature had been born. It occurred to me that I might compete for the title of Grandpa Moses of Chicano literature, depending on how you define Chicano and literature. So in 1980 I got around to copying what verses I had not destroyed in 1960, arranging them in chronological order. The surviving items ranged from early in 1930—when I was fourteen years of age—to the recent past, when I should have known better.

They were a formidable pile, no garden of verses by any means but more like an overgrown clearing in the chaparral, with more burrs and thistles than flowers. To weed out that tangled patch I decided to borrow a strategy from Border politics as I remembered them from the 1930s, namely the *menos pior* principle. When elections came round in my *patria chica*, one might hear exchanges like the following between *compadres* as they savored a few bottles of 3.2 at one of the local bars. Assuming, of course, that they had got their poll taxes on their own.

—Oiga, compadre, ¿por quién va a votar usted?—

—Pos la verdá que no sé, compadre. Tan cabrón está el pinto como el colorado.—

—Pero hay que votar, compadre. Vamos a pensarle un poco, a ver cuál de los dos es el menos pior.—

I looked around for a colleague willing to take time from his academic labors to help me decide which of my *versitos* were the least worst. Professor Ramón Saldívar of the UT English Department, whose judgment I respect, was good enough to accede to my request. He read my manuscript, and we agreed to meet in a few days to discuss his choices. This was in 1981. But time has a way of slipping beyond our reach before we know it. When I again gave serious thought to the matter, the few days had become eight years. I got in touch with Ramón Saldívar once more, and he was generous enough to read the whole manuscript a second time and to give me a typewritten list of the selections he thought were publishable.

I owe Ramón Saldívar my deepest gratitude for the time he spent on this excessively drawn-out project of mine. He made its termination possible, but he cannot be held responsible for the outcome. I have used his advice to make my own choices.

To my Border *pariente*, novelist Rolando Hinojosa, my

warmest appreciation for having suggested the title and epigraph of this work.

I am aware that if this volume finds any favor with the reader it will be mostly as a historical document. It is thus that I offer it, as the scribblings of a "proto-Chicano" of a half-century ago.

Américo Paredes
1989

Between Two Worlds

The Rio Grande

Muddy river, muddy river,
Moving slowly down your track
With your swirls and counter-currents,
As though wanting to turn back,

As though wanting to turn back
Towards the place where you were born,
While your currents swirl and eddy,
While you whisper, whimper, mourn;

So you wander down your channel
Always on, since it must be,
Till you die so very gently
By the margin of the sea.

All my pain and all my trouble
In your bosom let me hide,
Drain my soul of all its sorrow
As you drain the countryside,

For I was born beside your waters,
And since very young I knew
That my soul had hidden currents,
That my soul resembled you,

Troubled, dark, its bottom hidden
While its surface mocks the sun,
With its sighs and its rebellions,
Yet compelled to travel on.

When the soul must leave the body,
When the wasted flesh must die,

[handwritten margin notes: never ending flow – grows tiresome – No real home – displacement – wandering the world]

[handwritten margin note: Traveling soul]

I shall trickle forth to join you,
In your bosom I shall lie;

We shall wander through the country
Where your banks in green are clad,
Past the shanties of rancheros,
By the ruins of old Bagdad,

Till at last your dying waters,
Will release their hold on me,
And my soul will sleep forever
By the margin of the sea.[1]

—1934

Night on the Flats

Hushed is the owl in the chaparral
As the moon rises from the sea,
Making the dwarfed mesquitès tall . . .
    The White Woman walks in the moonlight.

Not a coyotè howls tonight,
It is a night of mystery,
Even the wind has died
    Of fright.

Even the stars so far above
Blink their little eyes in terror too,
While the lonely sage beneath the moon
Weeps glimmering tears of dew.
    The White Woman walks in the moonlight.

—1934

Africa

Africa! Africa!
Black soul with a song
And a chain.

Africa! Africa!
Black soul with a long
Cry of pain.

Carved piece of jade,
Soft beauty made
In the depths of the jungle's fierce breast

To the music of drums,
Of the tremulous drums,
Of the live, sobbing drums . . .

Of the drums!
Of the drums!!
Of the drums!!!
That incite such a curious unrest.

Africa! Africa!
Bare back burden-bent,
Choked cry in the night.

Africa! Africa!
Bare back that has felt
The whip of the white.

But in spite of the chains
The song remains,
I can hear it go echoing yet

To the rolling of drums,
Of the ominous drums,
Of the live, throbbing drums . . .

    Of the drums!
    Of the drums!!
    Of the drums!!!

May you never forget.

—1935

If You Let Me Kiss Your Lips

Down in Andalusia, in a painted gypsy camp,
While the sun is going out like some enormous
    lamp,
A belated traveler, his senses gone awhirl,
Whispers very softly to an Andalusian girl:
"*Ea*, Spanish gypsy of the lithe and swaying hips,
Twenty shining *duros* if you let me kiss your lips.
Let your lover nurse the jealous pangs he now
    must feel;
I am from Toledo and I have Toledo's steel.
You will have a score of such admirers, pretty
    witch;
You will flaunt before them in the trappings of
    the rich;
I shall buy you earrings of the finest that are
    made,
Bracelets, high *peinetas*, and a mile of gold bro-
    cade.
You will be a lady to your very finger-tips;
Ea, Spanish gypsy, if you let me kiss your lips!"

So spoke men in the jolly days of old,
When women could be won with a little blood
    and gold.
But what have I to give you, oh tremendous love
    of mine?
A tender sigh? A lock of hair? A pretty valen-
    tine?
I am but a poet, and my muse is starved and thin;
Spavined is my Pegasus, my lyre is made of tin.
I have neither gold nor fame nor anything to
    give;

Work? But I'm too lazy! As for war, I'd rather
    live.
I have but a ditty that inanely trips and skips:
That I'll gladly give you ... if you let me kiss
    your lips.

—1935

Ahí nomás

"Indian, dark brother from whose ancestors
Half of my father's fathers sprang,
You who know all of these ragged mountains,
Up to the nests that the eagles hang,

"Where do your weary footsteps take you?
In what strange place will you spend the night?
Indian, bronze Indian, sad beast of burden
Traveling on through the crumbling light."

Long was the road that he had to travel,
Difficult, rocky his journey was,
But with a shrug and a smile he answered,
"Just over there. *Sí ahí nomás.*"

For so the ages have taught the Indian
To mask his bitterness and despair;
His way is long but he bravely travels,
And all his goals are "just over there."

I too must travel among the mountains,
Searching the peaks for a distant dream,
Walking alone, with my eyes raised upward,
Up to the heights, where the eagles scream.

Should I encounter along my journey
A sister soul that is drawn to me,
Who rhymes with me in a perfect couplet,
Whose voice is pitched on my selfsame key,

Touching my arm, she will stop me, ask me,
"Where are you going? *¿A dónde vas?*"
And with a shrug and a smile I'll answer,
I too shall answer, *"Ahí nomás."*

—1935

Bolero

Under the tall mesquitè's shadow,
Amid the rustle of the palm trees,
Who could resist the hot temptation
Of her brown and Indian flesh?

Dancing the beat of a bolero
And in her naked arms imprisoned,
I kissed her lips, a purple blossom
Whose perfume is ever fresh.

—1935

Flute Song

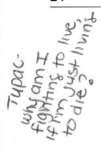

Tupac-
why am I
fighting to live,
if I'm just living
to die?

Why was I ever born — strong beginning
Heir to a people's sorrow,   — stop + think
Wishing this day were done   — already feel the
And yet fearful for the morrow.   pains

Why was I ever born
Proud of my southern race,
If I must seek my sun
In an Anglo-Saxon face.

Wail, wail, oh flutes, your dismal tune,
The agony of our birth;
Better perhaps had I never known
That you lived upon the earth.

—1935

At Night

During my hours of wakefulness,
When I wait for sleep in ambush,
   Then they come,
They come and stand around my bed
   In silence,
They do not move,
They do not speak nor point
   Accusing fingers.

They only stand,
   They stand
And watch me with lackluster eyes.

—1935

• vernacular dialect

The Mexico-Texan

Mex-Texans
– different from Mexicans

The Mexico-Texan he's one fonny man
Who leeves in the region that's north of the Gran',
Of Mexican father he born in these part,
And sometimes he rues it dip down in he's heart.

land, language, displacement, citizenship
identity

For the Mexico-Texan he no gotta lan',
He stomped on the neck on both sides of the Gran',
The dam gringo lingo he no cannot spik,
It twisters the tong and it make you fill sick.
A cit'zen of Texas they say that he ees,
But then, why they call him the Mexican Grease?
Soft talk and hard action, he can't understan',
The Mexico-Texan he no gotta lan'.

"citizen" but called a "greaser"
has no PROPERTY

fragmented
Mex/Texans not wanted in Mexico – identity

If he cross the reever, eet ees just as bad,
On high poleeshed Spanish he break up his had,
American customs those people no like,
They hate that Miguel they should call him El Mike,
And Mexican-born, why they jeer and they hoot,
"Go back to the gringo! Go lick at hees boot!"
In Texas he's Johnny, in Mexico Juan,
But the Mexico-Texan he no gotta lan'.

"got no HOME"

Being used, manipulated

Elactions come round and the gringos are loud,
They pat on he's back and they make him so proud,
They give him mezcal and the barbacue meat,
They tell him, "Amigo, we can't be defeat."
But efter election he no gotta fran',
The Mexico-Texan he no gotta lan'.

"has no VOICE"

Except for a few with their cunning and craft
? He count just as much as a nought to the laft,

[handwritten: Burden → doing all the work because he has nothing for himself.]

And they say everywhere, "He's a burden and drag,
He no gotta country, he no gotta flag."
He no gotta voice, all he got is the han'
To work like the burro; he no gotta lan'.

And only one way can his sorrows all drown,
He'll get drank as hell when next payday come roun',
For he has one advantage of all other man,
Though the Mexico-Texan he no gotta lan',
He can get him so drank that he think he will fly
Both September the Sixteen and Fourth of July.[2]

—1935

[handwritten: Dual identities difficulties to Be "American" Mexican-Texan + "Mexican" Mexican.]

Moonlight on the Rio Grande

The moon is so bright it dazzles me
To look her in the eye,
She lies like a round, bright pebble
On the dark-blue velvet sky,
She hangs like a giant pebble
In the star-incrusted sky.

The Rio Grande is bent and brown
And slow, like an aged peon,
But silver the lazy wavelets
Which the bright moon shines upon,
As bright as the little silver bells
On the round hat of a peon.

—1935

[handwritten notes: "compare + contrast"; "every cloud has its silver lining"]

Guitarreros

Bajaron el toro prieto,
que nunca lo habían bajado ...

Black against twisted black
The old mesquite (thicket)
Rears up against the stars
Branch bridle hanging,
While the bull comes down from the mountain
Driven along by your fingers,
Twenty nimble stallions prancing up and down
      the *redil* of the guitars.

quick + light in motion

One leaning on the trunk, one facing—
Now the song:
Not cleanly flanked, not pacing,
But in a stubborn yielding that unshapes
And shapes itself again,
Hard-mouthed, zigzagged, thrusting,
Thrown not sung
One to the other.

The old man listens in his cloud
Of white tobacco smoke.
"It was so," he says,
"In the old days it was so."[3]

3 people

—1935

Doubt

The days go by.

Here is a hungry beast, a beast in pain
That feeds upon itself and lives again,
And it will never die.

Is it a wonder, then, this shapeless cry,
Irrevocable song
Under an empty sky?

So are the branches splayed,
The hunchback does not change for having prayed.

—1936

Winter in April

Dawn comes at last to my window sill,
  It's April
  Still
  The cold endures.

The rain on the eaves slowly drips and drips,
The morning wind brushes across my lips
  Like a kiss from yours.

  Dawn, wind, and rain,
  Ghosts of wasted summers.

—1936

Rose Petals

To you,
Love-soon-to-be-lost,
I bring you roses.

Men of today
Are tired, they say,
Of yesterday's artificialities;
They want to sing of the truth,
    The truth
With formalities;
They want to sing of the naked truth
    And its realities.

So if I sing
Of your sweet face,
    Your quiet grace,
Of the golden glintings of your hair,
    Of the little gestures
    That make you fair
    To my lover's eyes,
Then men will say that my songs are lies.

But I cannot sing of your pliant waist,
Of your warm and naked flesh,
Of your citron breasts tipped with trembling rose,
Of your lean yet swelling hips;
I cannot sing, though these things I know,
For you do not move me so.

    If love is lust
    I do not love you then.
You make some men as lecherous as beasts in must,

But you do not stir
These brothel passions in my flesh;
My spirit does not hold such a consuming fire,
Such passion is not mine.
    You stir instead
    Within my breast
A certain vague and sad desire
For something that I never had
And I shall never have,
    A sad, sad longing
    That is almost pain
For something that I one day was
    And wish to be again.

    Yet, I'm no pure,
    No light-filled soul,
No mystic zealot whose treasured goal
    Is Heaven's gates;
    I am no lofty, pious mind,
    No paragon of good,
I'm just as greedy and as lewd
    As all my kind,
    That crawl forlorn,
Little above the other beasts they scorn,
    Upon this ball
Of dust and stones and filth.

    Other women
    Have stirred me deep,
For after all I am mostly beast,
A brute that entrapped in a web of dreams
    Growls in his sleep.
    And again,
I have seen other men when they look on you,

I have seen their eyes
Shine with a glow
Such as the lights that over the swamps
Waver and go.

But you do not stir me so,
Though that be there
It lies at rest
When I have you near.
You stir instead within my breast
A certain vague and sad desire
For something I have never had
And I shall never have,
A sad, sad longing
That is almost pain
For something that I one day was
And wish to be again.

—1936

Alma pocha

Alma pocha
ensangrentada,
la sufrida,
la olvidada,
la rebelde sin espada;
alma pocha
salpicada
de tragedia y humorada,
alma pocha.

En tu propio terruño serás extranjero
por la ley del fusil y la ley del acero;
y verás a tu padre morir balaceado
por haber defendido el sudor derramado;
verás a tu hermano colgado de un leño
por el crimen mortal de haber sido trigueño.
Y si vives, acaso, será sin orgullo,
con recuerdos amargos de todo lo tuyo;
tus campos, tus cielos, tus aves, tus flores
serán el deleite de los invasores;
para ellos su fruto dará la simiente,
donde fueras el amo serás el sirviente.
Y en tu propio terruño serás extranjero
por la ley del fusil y la ley del acero.

De este modo
habló el destino
en la jornada tejana
¡y la boca se envilece
con el nombre de Santa Anna!
Alma pocha
vas llorando

la vergüenza mexicana.

Alma pocha,
alma noble y duradera,
la que sufre,
la que espera.[4]

—1936

Coplas

Mi vida, cuando te vistas
de esa manera,
no vayas al camposanto—
no vayas, güera;

que si los muertos miraran
tanta hermosura
dejarían todititos
la sepultura.

—1936

Tres faces del pocho
Comedia en Tres Autos, Modelo T

Tableau I: *The Passionate Spaniard*.

Scene is announced by a flourish of heraldic trumpets,
which shift into a snappy *paso doble* as the lights come up.
He is sitting there, facing front, his trousers around his an-
kles, on a toilet seat in a cheap hotel room in Mexico City.
He came as a tourist to see La Gran Tenochtitlán, site of
great deeds by his ancestors, *los conquistadores*. After a
weekend of tacos, whores, and mariachis, we find him en-
throned on the crapper, spilling out his guts and suffering
the torments not of the damned but of the *gademes*. He has
been called a *pocho*, has paid three or four *mordidas*, and
finally had his wallet stolen. When we first see him he is
staring at the floor, head in hands, elbows on knees. Now
he lifts his head and looks out front into empty space. The
trumpets bray out a final flourish and then subside to a faint
background music as he begins to speak, bitter disillusion-
ment in his voice.

> Raza gloriosa y real de mis abuelos,
> ¡oh, mi raza giganta!
> que aplastaste en el polvo con tu planta
> ¡cuánto guerrero altivo!
> que cruzaste los montes y los mares
> llevando dondequiera tus altares,
> y en tu lenguaje dulce y expresivo
> el oro vivo.
>
> Leona de los ibéricos castillos,
> madre de leones,
> sangre de aquellos ínclitos campeones
> de gesto varonil y férreos brillos,

raza conquistadora,
viéndote ahora
sé bien que en estas playas
se ha apagado tu flama bienhechora;
y mientras tú desmayas,
de aquestos tus escombros ¿qué ha salido?
¡un pueblo degenerado y maldecido!

Pueblo bastardo que parió Malinche,
ciego por el poder, servil al oro,
pueblo sin tradiciones ni decoro
prendido al presupuesto como chinche;
amas más al maguey que al mismo trigo
y para conseguir mejor la vida
tienes como tu lema *La Mordida*
y es tu blasón la mano del mendigo.

¡Pueblo de los farsantes y holgazanes!
¡Pueblo de caciquillos y tarzanes!
Gente de intriga:
tus triunfos más brillantes son traiciones
y elevas como héroes a matones.

Vives con la inmundicia cara a cara,
si el mundo rueda o no ¿qué te importara?
Llena de cualquier modo la barriga,
te sientas a rascar—¡Dios te maldiga!

With shaking hand he reaches for the roll of toilet paper, as the lights fade.

Tableau II: *The Second-Generation* Exiliado.

Lights rise to the music of "La Zandunga" played on violins and marimbas. We see the outside brick wall of an apartment in Chicago, in the center of which is a large bedroom window. He is leaning his elbows on the sill, his dreamy gaze fixed on the distance, front. Behind and to the side can be glimpsed an old-fashioned spring phonograph, and beyond, on the closet door, a tuxedo jacket. He has just taken his Gringa date home, after trying unsuccessfully to make her in the back seat of a friend's car. Restless, he tries to take his mind off her by thinking about his beloved Mexico, a country he has never visited. His father once was a Mexican consul and then a refugee who raised a family in exile. The family talks about going back for good, but they never go even for a visit. The window out of which he leans faces south, and he fantasizes that the slight breeze that plays over his face comes directly from Mexico. He even imagines he can smell the flowers from the *jardín de flores* that is Mexico above the exhaust fumes and the faint smell that reaches his neighborhood from Chicago's famous stockyards. The violins and marimbas fade into the background as he begins to speak, eyes still in the distance.

> Déjame que te cante, patria amada,
> un canto de esperanza y de tristeza
> que lleve sueños de oro del mañana
> y místicos anhelos de poeta;
>
> déjame que te cante un himno extraño
> lleno de carcajadas y suspiros
> para que sepas bien lo desdichados
> que pueden ser los hijos de tus hijos.
>
> México, eres tú la tierra santa,
> la tierra prometida,
> hacia la cual he vuelto yo los ojos
> desde mis primeros días,
> donde las flores tienen más perfume,
> donde las aguas son más cristalinas,

y donde son más grandes los racimos
que cuelgan en las viñas;
amo tus aromáticos cantares
como la flor de tiesto ama a la brisa
y sueño con tus montes y tus lagos
como se sueña con la bienquerida;
feliz si un día mis ardientes ojos
por fin te miran
y estos mis pies, a tu terruño extraños,
tu tierra pisan
para pasar por todas tus praderas
como la golondrina
y beberme tus múltiples bellezas
con las lágrimas mías,
para poder erguirme bajo el cielo,
dando la voz bravía,
y gritar para que oiga el mundo entero:
—¡Esta es la tierra mía! ...
... El llanto viene cálido a mis ojos,
cálidas en mis ojos son las lágrimas
como si mis anhelos congelados
por el frío mortal de la distancia
al fuego abrasador se derritieran
y en copioso caudal se derramaran.

Es la noche chinaca con rebozo
bordado de luciérnagas y estrellas,
el mundo es campamento donde sólo
se ve pasar la luna, sentinela,
y yo que me desvelo vuelvo el rostro
hacia el sur, donde estás bendita tierra;
y así como el que de un elíxir bebe,
así aspiro tu brisa fresca y suave,
la brisa que del suelo tuyo viene,

la que ha agitado el fuego de tus lares,
tu brisa, la envidiada, la dichosa
porque ha llegado a todos tus parajes,
holgándose en la nieve de tus montes,
jugando con las flores de tus valles;
tu brisa, tan gentil y perfumada
como uno de tus típicos cantares,
de esos de mucho amor y valentía,
de esos llenos de angustia y de nostalgia,
de esos que se querellan por las penas
que nacen al calor de una mirada,
de esos cantares tristes y dolientes
que se cantan de noche a las muchachas;
así en la noche, al aspirar tu brisa,
pienso otra vez en ti, tierra soñada,
sueño en un porvenir lleno de gloria
como se sueña en la mujer que se ama,
y bajo el embozo negro de la noche
se me hacen otra vez los ojos lágrimas.

He turns from the window toward the phonograph and hunts among the records on the table beside it as the background music switches from "La Zandunga" to "Canción Mixteca." Exasperated: "Now, where the hell is that song?" Shrugs and picks a record and puts it on the phonograph. "Canción Mixteca" is abruptly cut off, and a jazz band blares out "St. Louis Blues." He snaps his fingers and sings: "Now, if it weren't for powder, and for store-bought hair . . . " The lights fade.

Tableau III: El Poeta Pocho

The scene is a little rundown 3.2 beer joint on the border: *los agachados*. The bar is in the rear, facing front. Lights come up to the tune of a very fast polka played by

Chicho Martínez (El Huracán del Valle) on a wheezy old accordion, accompanied by a *bajo* player who is obviously having trouble keeping up with Chicho. El Poeta Pocho is facing the bar, with his back to the audience. He needs a haircut, his shoes are run down at the heels, and there is a big patch on the seat of his pants. Abruptly he turns round, facing the audience and leaning back on the bar. The music changes to a slow, stately *chotis* played by El Cuarteto Aguilar (Los Vagabundos). After a few bars, the music fades into the background as he begins to speak.

> Canto al coraje heroico, a la ira de una raza,
> a la altivez que abraza y que enciende el corazón;
> canto al odio titánico de hazañas mil pletórico,
> ese rencor histórico que es casi religión.
> Bajo su acerbo látigo los pueblos se han formado,
> sus fauces han desgarrado cadáveres sin fin;
> está su voz en la trompa, estridente, bronca y
>   brusca
> del adalid que busca derechos y botín.
>
> Canto al deber de sangre, al instinto del orgullo
> del cual para lo suyo,
> ¡canto a la tradición!

He has begun speaking in a low, measured voice, but his speech gets faster and louder until he is shouting at this point.

> Que mi voz sea el grito torturado
> del clarín de alerta,
> y lo repetirán todos los ecos:
> ¡De pie! ¡Despierta!
>
> ¡Que desaten sus ásperos bramidos
> trompas de guerra,

que olor a sangre y no perfume a rosas
cubra la tierra ... !

Stops and looks over one shoulder, then the other, apparently embarrassed by his own rhetoric. Resumes in a calmer tone but again his voice rises.

No le canto a Cuauhtémoc, no le canto a Pelayo,
Al Cid y a Moctezuma no les he cantado yo;
El Cortez de quien hablo en Tejas nació.

Yo le canto a Pizaña, yo le canto a Cortina,
a Jacinto Treviño y a Gregorio Cortez,
los viriles campeones de una raza transida
que aunque triste y caída no se deja vencer.

Paladines inmensos de razgos heroicos,
guerreros enormes, cautivos estoicos
que hasta el fin ondularon el hispano pendón,
caballeros andantes que molinos retaron
y el furor desdeñaron del anglosajón;
éstos son los hidalgos
a los que canto yo.

Echo backstage repeats mockingly, "¡Yo! ¡Yo! ¡Yo! ¡Yo!" He looks out over the audience, as though seeking the speaker there. When he speaks again his voice is intense but controlled.

¡Sí! ¡Yo!

Pues soy de los vendidos por Santa Anna,
llevo en mis venas
todo el dolor y las antiguas penas
de la raza mexicana
cuya sangre derrochó demente

esa mano tirana
entre un rato de siesta en San Jacinto
y un toque de diana.

Con aquella hetacombe cesaron mis brillos,
me vi esclavizado y cargado de grillos,
mis ojos altivos perdieron la luz;
y aún sufro mil muertes por llegar a Angostura,
he comido traición y he bebido amargura,
en Chapultepec he muerto y también en Ver-
    acruz.

¿Y quién eres tú?

In the background the polka takes over from the *chotis*.
Lights begin to fade, but very slowly. He looks fixedly out
over the audience, as if too moved to say anymore. Then he
seems to focus directly on one person, and he says: "¡Oye,
cabrón! ¿Y qué chingados me ves?" Polka music comes on
full blast as the lights go out.

—1936

A Licha

Si en el cielo sajón del cristianismo
    hay ángeles morenos
como tu cara son, tenlo sabido,
    las caras de ellos.
Como tu cara, sí, como tu cara,
que en este camino oscuro
    me iluminara.

—1937

A orillas del Bravo

La brisa que se queja entre la rama
acaba con el día calcinante
y esparce sobre el agua murmurante
aromas de amapola y de retama;

los cielos que hace poco fueran llama
se han tornado en estuche de diamante,
ya del mundo la frente palpitante
el beso de la noche la embalsama;

del chaparral lejano brota un trino:
es el zinzontli en melodía plena
que vierte su gorjeo cristalino

y en noches cuando está la luna llena
¡cuántas veces te he visto, Pan divino,
jugando con las ninfas en la arena!

—1937

Mi pueblo

—A mi barrio, El Cuatro Veintiuno.
—A mi amigo, Sabas Klahn.

Pueblo mío, pueblo mío, multiforme caserío
recostado junto al río bajo el gris amanecer,
junto al río lento y bruno tienes barrios uno a
     uno
y entre tantos el "Veintiuno",
el que a mí me vio crecer.

Pueblo lleno de lisonjas por palmeras y toronjas,
con tus frailes y tus monjas y tu iglesia colonial,
con quebrantos y quereres, con cantinas y mu-
     jeres,
y con todos los placeres
de pecado capital.

Tú que cruento y pervertido de mis penas te has
     reído
porque incógnito y caído me contemplas, pueblo
     vil;
tú que en dulce nigromancia me arrullaste allá
     en mi infancia,
y me diste tu fragancia,
pueblo vívido y gentil.

Tienes fuertes y raquíticos, hipócritas y críticos,
tienes líderes políticos que te compran con mez-
     cal,
tienes bailes y conciertos, hay riquezas en tus
     huertos,
llegan naves a tus puertos
por el cielo y por el mar.

Con tus blancas carreteras las distancias aligeras,
tus lozanas gringas güeras son marfil, oro y azur;
y en tus fiestas y verbenas luces vírgenes more-
nas
que tus risas y tus penas
han soñado desde el sur.

Eres cierta incertidumbre entre cielo y podre-
dumbre,
del abismo y de la cumbre el destino te formó
citadino y campirano, eres yanqui-mexicano,
eres méxico-texano,
¡eres pocho, como yo!

Ah, mi pueblo, no lo ignoro; yo soy pardo, in-
coloro,
mas cual pájaro canoro llevo un canto dentro
mí;
ese canto que me llena con su aroma de azu-
cena,
aunque seas "tierra ajena",
ese canto es para ti.

Porque a mí me importa un bledo que me apun-
ten con el dedo,
que de mí murmure quedo tu correcta sociedad;
pueblo bajo y barullero, pueblo dulce y roman-
cero,
yo te juro que te quiero,
yo te quiero de verdad.[5]

—1937

El barco velero

El barco velero se aleja, se aleja allá en lontanan-
    za
en mares azules como son los sueños de amor y
    esperanza,
cual franjas de espuma se pierden sus velas en
    esa distancia;
y viéndolas quiero
ser barco velero
en aguas lejanas.

Por eso he nacido aquí donde el Bravo y el Golfo
    se abrazan,
mi espíritu niño creció con las brisas que besan
    las playas,
y a veces escucho una voz en el viento que canta
    y me llama;
y oyéndola quiero
ser barco velero
en aguas lejanas.

—1937

Voz en la obscuridad

Voz en la obscuridad que vas cantando
una canción de luces y alegría
sin pensar en que tarda el nuevo día
¿vendrá el amanecer? ¡Quién sabe cuándo!

—1938

Sueños del Sur

Allá en aquella escondida tierra de Yucatán,
tierra de dioses, de golondrinas y del faisán,
hay una joven que a mí me espera
y es más hermosa que la quimera
que sorprendiera al rudo Canek en el Mayapán.

Mis horas tristes y desoladas terminarán,
las azucenas y los jazmines florecerán,
el día loco de mi partida
rumbo a la tierra desconocida,
rumbo a la tierra dulce y soñada de Yucatán.

Allá en la tierra de los venados, en Mazatlán,
donde las rítmicas pescadoras vienen y van,
una doncella me está esperando
sobre una barca y está cantando:
"Las olas vienen, las olas vienen y lo traerán".

No seas necio, febril poeta, seudogalán,
nadie te espera en aquellas tierras de Yucatán,
nadie te espera en extrañas playas
bajo la sombra de templos mayas,
nadie te espera sobre la proa
junto a las playas de Sinaloa,
nadie te espera en el lindo puerto de Mazatlán.

—1938

A César Augusto Sandino

Cinco años después de su muerte

Las selvas fueron tu mejor escudo,
alma indomable de jaguar suriano,
todo el poder del norteamericano
ceder no quiso ni vencerte pudo.

Empuñando el acero ya desnudo
el mañoso sajón volvióse fiera,
quiso que la justicia enmudeciera;
y en el combate rudo

tú desdeñaste el yugo. Yo te canto,
yo que he llorado y he sufrido tanto
el yugo colectivo de mi raza.

Vives aún y vivirás, Sandino,
más allá del furor del asesino
y del fragor que ya nos amenaza.

—1939

Pensando en ti, William Tell

Quién fuera montaraz.
Sólo en las peñas
podría haber lugar para el latino;
este sajón endino
todo aniquila
y donde no conquista pos se cuela
aunque no tenga vela
en ese entierro,
nomás de purito perro
o por volar la huila.

¡Pero ni señas
de un cerro!

—1939

Lines to be Read Over
My Sixty-Fifth Birthday

When I was young I wrote great poesy
Grander than Milton, sweeter than Shakespeare
Was my impassioned sonnetry
    Or so I thought
    Others did not
    Oh painful memory
Life could have been quite tough
But for a girl, she read the stuff
    That was enough for me.

—1940

Carolina

In the seven hours of darkness
When the owl and the cricket cry,
Up and down the ranks of my gray, gray thoughts
Your name goes singing by.

It goes singing, singing, singing
A sad old Hispanic song,
And the song will not cease, will not cease until
My heart is still.

—1940

Última cena

He de volver a ti, calladamente,
como vuelve a su cueva la raposa,
como vuelve al abismo la corriente,
una tarde color de mariposa;

pues no se me concede el olvidarme
de la noche que hicimos misa loca
con el pan extasiado de tu carne
y la copa escarlata de tu boca.

Mas trajo el alba su fatal contraste;
con el beso de Judas me dejaste.

He de volver a ti ...

—1940

The Four Freedoms

Raza (handwritten)

Lengua, Cultura, Sangre:—
es vuestro mi cantar,
sois piedra de los mares
y muro del hogar;
este país de "Cuatro Libertades"
nada nos puede dar.

Justicia ... ¿acaso existe?
La fuerza es la justicia,
palabras humorísticas: Justicia y Libertad.
Nos queda sólo la Raza,   *different* (handwritten)
nos queda sólo la Lengua;   *language* (handwritten)
hay que guardarlas siempre
y mantenerlas vivas
por una eternidad.[6]

—1941

(handwritten left margin, rotated): There is no justice + liberty. All we have are our people + our language. We must guard + maintain them for an eternity, these always.

Hastío

Nunca temí el dolor, sólo temía
que el corazón, cansado de sufrir,
insensible por fin en algún día
dejara de sentir.

Por eso fui soberbio y fui ladino
y débil, pues caí cobardemente
en la zanja a lo largo del camino
y me manché de fango pestilente.

En la negra tormenta que me abruma
soy el ala extraviada, que abatida,
no puede mucho más llevar a cuestas
la bajeza y el tedio de la vida.

—1941

Adiós a un soldado

Amigo, querido amigo
¡que te mantenga el gobierno!
Pues si te vas a la guerra
sales también de este infierno
de esquinas y serenatas
(¡los sábados, chicaspatas!)
y también la borrachera;
eso ni es vida siquiera.

    Que te vaya bien, te digo,
pues por aquí apesta a cuerno.

    Lo que hubiera sucedido,
quedándote en este vicio,
es que estarías bien jodido
pa' cuando cobres tu juicio;
como humano desperdicio
rodando te hubieras ido,
ni un pie derecho ni un quicio
ya te hubieran sostenido
aunque fueras maderero;
ciertos poetas vulgares
que les gusta el lero-lero
recorrerían los bares
recordando tus romances
con las lindas,
con la bellas,
con tus amantes aquellas
de bocas guindas—
la compañía
que alegró tus penas
de mediodía.

¡Ah, las morenas!

    —1942

Primavera

Llueve obstinadamente sobre el campo
    en el cuarto mes,
se hincha la semilla ingerminada
    de un tentativo ayer;
abril, abril ¿qué tienen tus mañanas?
¡cómo empapan la paja de los años
    con gotitas de hiel!

—1942

La libertad

Raza morena y mestiza
¡oh, semilla de grandeza!
llevas en ti la entereza
que te da la juventud.
Y esa pobreza afanosa
no es maldición, es un reto;
es el desecho del feto,
no pudrición de ataúd.

Indio descalzo, trigueño,
que llorando vas tu suerte,
indio, ¡qué diera por verte
soberano de verdad!
Con el estómago lleno,
bien vestido y bien calzado
y en tu destino confiado—
ésa es la libertad.

—1942

Cuento corto

—Paredes, poeta sois, así naciste
no has podido calmar tu sufrimiento
con el vano placer que recogiste
de este mundo podrido y purulento.

—Tú de la gloria y el placer sediento
el burdel de la vida recorriste
y por fin te cansó ser hoja al viento,
ya encontraste la paz, ¿por qué estás triste?

—No me digas, por Dios, sé bien tu pena,
añoras el laúd y el verde estero
y la flauta forjada con avena;

—es que quieres volver a ser coplero,
no sufras más esa fatal condena,
ven otra vez a mí, que yo te espero.—

Así me habló mi musa cierto día cuando la pobrecita venía
—venía a molestarme con eso de querer embaucarme a vol-
ver a la dulce poesía. Yo no quería. Eso de la ilusión y
el desengaño son cosas del antaño —yo decía— los tiem-
pos no permiten tales cosas; esas disertaciones amorosas
... ¡disparates! ¡desvaríos! ¿y saldrían ayer de labios míos?
Me responde la musa: —Canta, canta; mira, que si tuvieras
una planta ... ¿Planta? le contesté con loca furia a lo que
parecióme ser injuria:

—Ya no tengo ni suela en el zapato,
mucho menos poética plantilla,
en cantarle al Dios Pan (con mantequilla)
hace tiempo me estoy pasando el rato.

—No me vengas aquí con tanto guato,

oh musa de mi edad temprana y pilla,
el sudor del trabajo te mancilla,
tengo que trabajar, ¡destino ingrato!

—Ni te acerques a mí con triste lloro:
tu numen es dorado, pero ... ¿es oro?
Aléjate de mí, visión incauta,

—mira que ya la tripa me reniega,
no se mantiene con avena griega,
¡vete muy lejos a tocar tu flauta!—

Se fue la musa, se fue llorando, y era su llanto como un can-
tar, cual eco triste que el alma hiere de algo que muere en
la obscuridad.

—1942

Monólogo

Silencios almidonados
caminos sin asentar
pensamientos lavados sin jabón
penas de dos por cuatro
 ¿es la vida combustión?

Febriles intoxicantes cerebrales
combustiones heterogenéticas y suaves
ruidos estrepitosos de pájaros que se van
 no volverán
el itinerario poemático no lo puede permitir
 jamás.

¿Es superególatra el mundo de Adán?
Eva es hipocondríaca
 por eso hay un Dios.

Los tendones de la vida
se estiran hasta cierto punto
 y nada más.

En el inmenso hangar de tu recuerdo
ya no está el avión
de la ilusión
pero el espíritu eléctrico
es teléfono del cosmos
y nada es inútil
ni el cinematógrafo
y hasta los automóviles
y los mórbidos hallazgos
de la revista *Life*.

     —1942

Lines For a Birthday Card

Oh, muse that once inspired Shakespeare
And made Ben Jonson rare,
Abide with me while I indite
A song for lady fair.

This is her birthday, gentle muse,
And may God bless her mother
For bringing her into the world,
She ain't quite like no other.

So let us wish her many years
Without the curse of old age,
And let us hope that this won't make
Her go into a cold rage.

(For she can be a little odd),
Let's wish her joy unbounded
(She wants to die an aerial death—
I think she should be grounded!)

Let's also wish her happiness,
It can't be bought for money;
And let us hope the world for her
Will not be sad but funny.

Let's wish her health and wealth and love
And champagne when she's thirsty—
Hell! This is dragging out too much,
Let's just say, "Happy Birthday."

—1943

Pa′ qué

¿A qué luchar con brazo furibundo
en contra del infiel en la cruzada,
o navegar en pos de un nuevo mundo
para el retoño de la raza amada?

¡Si no les importa una triste chingada
de nada, de nada!

—1943

Tango Negro

Quisiera que mis versos fueran
casas abandonadas por mi mujer,
quisiera que mis versos fueran
a chupar los melocotones del ayer.

Forjo en el yunque de mi fantasía
de aves nocturnas la triste queja
y viene la realidad ¡o suerte impía!
en forma de mi vieja.

Tal vez a la vuelta del camino
me encuentre agazapada
a mi suegra, la malvada,
y el turbio río, mi destino,
que cruza mi sendero,
me traiga los de carnero.

Esto no es musa ni melancolía
ni tampoco es un quinqué,
es sólo una existencia entristecida,
pinche punto que jerré,
¡ah, la tragicomedia de la vida
si la que vino ayer ya no se fue![7]

—1943

Guitarras y mujeres

Con poco talento dije
en unas estrofas ralas
que las mujeres mentían
como las guitarras malas.

Contesta Matías Serrata:
—No estoy en tus pareceres,
di que mienten las guitarras
como las malas mujeres.—

Pos tiene sus asegunes,
y aquí la duda me agarra:
¿es cuestión del individuo?
¿la mujer? ¿o la guitarra?

—1943

Coplas

Morena, morena clara,
la de los ojos de noche,
la de la tez sonrosada,
la de los albos amores,

ven mírame a mí, morena
con esos ojos arteros
que alumbran mi noche oscura
como dos negros luceros.

En tu pelo saetinado
hay olor a primavera,
hay vino tinto en tus labios
y embriaguez en tus caderas.

Son tus senos juveniles
dos escondidos puñales;
se me han clavado en el pecho
y todo mi ser deshacen.

Morena, morena clara,
la de ojos de negra noche,
este mal de amor me mata
¡no quiero morir tan joven!

—1943

Aguafuerte estival

El sol de la tarde, cual viejo lascivo,
acaricia su cuerpo
con luz moribunda—ella exhala un suspiro
frente al gran espejo.

Sus ojos confusos
no miran de lleno
su cuerpo desnudo,

muslos sonrosados,
caderas redondas
y seno elevado

tiemblan como tiembla
una llama perdida
entre rojas tinieblas.

Y por el campo de sus ojos claros
pasan en estampida
los centauros.

—1944

Pipo's Song

The tide is at full, the dam has burst,
The world is tight like a fiddle,
It isn't the ends that hurt the most,
The hurt is worst in the middle.

For time is a four-letter word
And death is well-come tonic,
Love is a lingering ache in the crotch
And clinging to life is chronic.

                                    —1944

El reloj

Soñar . . . soñar . . . qué largos son los sueños . . .

     1 . . .
        2 . . .
            3 . . .
                2 . . .

así van cayendo los círculos negros
en un gigantesco reloj . . .

     . . . 3 . . .
          2 . . .
             1 . . .
                2 . . .

¿qué son los sonámbulos? ¿qué dice dormido
mi hermano? . . .

     . . . 3 . . .
          2 . . .

¿qué es el hombre al final, serafín o gusano?
y el sueño ¿qué es?

     . . . 3 . . .
          3 . . .

se boga, se boga en países lejanos . . .

     . . . 3 . . .
          2 . . .

¿es el sueño otra vida? ¿o es la muerte un sueño

y ese sueño Dios?

        ... 2 ...
            1 ...
                2 ...

En el universo hay un gran vacío
y en ese vacío palpita un reloj ...

        ... 1 ...
            2 ...

dentro del reloj hay un mar sin linderos
que ondea y retumba
por todos los evos ...

        ... 1 ...
            2 ...
                3 ...
                    2 ...

y en el mar inmenso hay sólo una nave
que también se mueve, ¿a dónde?
quién sabe ...

        ... 2 ...
            ... 2 ...
                ... 2 ...
                    ....2 ...

                        —1944

Insomnio

Voz de mis infinitas soledades ...

El insomnio es una bestia enjaulada,
una bestia negra que sufre un tormento porque
     está encerrada,
            v
                    a
                            e
                    n
                e
        i
v
        v
                a
buscando la oculta salida;
detrás de las rejas de mis nerviosidades
            v
                    a
                            e
                    n
                e
        i
v
        v
                a
buscando la oculta salida.

Me están matando en silencio y todos me mi-
     ran pero nadie sabe
          que me están matando.
Pasa la muerte, vestida de novia, cantando,
mientras que mi vida

        v
          a
               e
          n
        e
   i
v
    v
        a
buscando la oculta salida.

    Hay un dolor escondido en la noche, un dolor
      secreto,
Es una carcajada, es un grito demente que surge
      y que calla,
es un aullido que ha muerto, que ha muerto en
      la seca garganta
de agudo temblor sacudida,
buscando la oculta salida.

    Voz de mis infinitas soledades,
qué frágil es el incienso de todas la realidades;
detrás de la rejas el insomnio está,

        v
          a
               e
          n
        e
   i
v
    v
        a
buscando la oculta salida;

      v

        a

           e

        n

      e

   i

v

  v

   a

buscando la oculta salida.

En la obscuridad hay una caverna
y en esa caverna está un troglodita atizando un
    fuego que me quema el alma;
y de las orejas de la bestia negra dos zarcillos de
    oro se encuentran colgados;
dos senos erectos brotan de su pecho como blan-
    cos tlacotes
y tiemblan dos lágrimas en los dos pezones;
lágrima salobre y salobre la carne—

Ah, la bestia negra, bestia enfurecida,
que sigue buscando la oculta salida,
cuando la puerta se abra
    ¡ay de tu blanco cuello!
    ¡ay de tu sangre pálida!

—1944

Mercenaria

Era tan bella como un día de pago,
de esos de a fin de mes, cuando es preciso
pagar la renta, y la luz, y el agua;

y era rubia, de un rubio tan rojizo
como el cobre del que hacen los centavos
donde está Lincoln, dios del manumiso.

Y era tan blanca como la memoria
de aquel que debe y que pagar no quiso;

era tan bella como un día de pago
y por ser día de pago—pos se m'hizo.

—1944

Orange Grove

The white
orange blossoms
silver filigree lost
in the silent arms of the haze
and mist.

Again
the scent we loved
cloys like the days of youth
when the perfume was sweetest in
your breath.[8]

—1944

Oración del soldado

Lord God of Hosts,
Señor de Señores,
Dios de las escaramuzas
y los combates mayores:
reparte los cocolazos
como reparten los dólares
en nuestros pagos mensuales;
que sea la mayor parte
para nuestros oficiales.

De la ira feroz del sargento primero
líbrame, Señor, por piedad te lo ruego;
con las huestes de Tojo
me las veo yo solo.

—1945

Homecoming

I am homesick for a home I've never lived in,
A home
Made from the looks on soldiers' faces
Reading their letters after mail-call,
Made from the smiles that women give their men
In crowded buses and in railway stations,
Of such things is my dream home made.

There was a shy and pretty mother
Nursing her baby girl on a railway coach
Between Houston and Texarkana;
There was a man at whom his woman smiled
When we reached the station;
Her look made me lonely for this home
I've never lived in.

No matter if it is a poster pic
Cut out of *Homes and Gardens*.

—1945

In Memoriam
Manuel Cruz

¡Pobre Manuel!
Triste cantor aquel.
Ah, qué suerte le tocó.
Amó. Soñó. Murió.
Tal fue la historia de él.

—Okazaki, 1945

La tarde era triste

Tequila, mestizas y mariachis
vienen a llamarme con las quietas
noches glaciales:
mestizas, mariachis
y el sol de Brownsville.[9]

—Okazaki
1945

Pro Patria

In the mud huts of China,
The tile-roofed paper houses of Japan,
In the straw-thatched *jacales* of old Mexico,
The rain-blackened shacks of Arkansas,

Here is my fatherland, these are my people,
My beloved,
Black, yellow, brown—
And even if their eyes are blue—

These are my people,
The bleeding wounds upon the feet and hands
Of humankind.

And the sleek bastards in the swallowtails,
They who can say which course the earth shall
    take,
How it should swing on its axis,
The sons-of-bitches in the stripèd pants,

They have the awesome task
Of making this fatherland of mine
Flourish in filth, thrive in a grave of garbage,
So that some other day we all may perish
In one grand shout of glory.

It is for this we breed
More numerous
Than a triumphant soldier's dreams.

—Okazaki
1945

Japonesa

Japonesa, Japonesa
la del kimono de púrpura,
la de la mirada airosa,
japonesa, japonesa,
japonesa misteriosa:
hay en tus ojos extraños
una noche de amargura
y un piélago de dulzura,
naciste para el amor,
tienes el hierro candente
de belduques samurayes
y el perfume evanescente
de los cerezos en flor.

Mujer de esta raza antigua
como tus sierras azules,
te vistes de seda y tules
y sonríes tu dolor:
dame el exótico beso
de tu boquita de fresa,
la de los labios sensuales,
japonesa, japonesa
que sonríes tu dolor,
en tus brazos orientales
mitigaré mi destierro,
hija de sangre y de hierro
y de cerezos en flor.

—Okazaki
1946

Prayer

From caring too much
defend us
from love in excess
restore us
sunder us, sever us
from too much consciousness rend us
Whoever-You-Are.

—Gamagori
1946

To a WAC Officer

Major, major, gracious me!
Khaki skirt and nylon knee.
What dread hand can put your charms
Through the manual of arms?

Tell me, would you care to mention
How your tits stand at attention
While the rest goes swinging free:
   Hut!
       Two!
           Three!
Could he who made T-5 make thee?

If you're willing, I am ready,
Though your scent is sort of ... heady?
The things a man will do, alas,
For a piece of brass.

                  —Tokyo
                  1946

Song of the Gigolo

Listen!
Words to a ballad in a Tokyo bar
with my guitar.

With my guitar
I sing to you, bring to you
Songs about dreams misplaced and of distant
      sadnesses;
Girl of the blinding smile and the shiny car,
With my guitar.

Listen!
You are blonde and beautiful
Like the sun when it shines through ice,
Striking a thousand colors at once,
Firing them, painting them, setting them all aflame
Till the cold has become iridescence,
So shall I be to your northern eyes
With my guitar.

I shall touch with summer the winter sky
That is in your eyes
Giving them warmth and splendor,
To the golden sunlight of your hair
I shall bring the cool and the tropic night
Of an ancient tragedy.

Listen!
I will tell you the joys and the pain
And the warm, soft secrets of my swarthy race,
I shall paint you the thousand colors of a *sarape*
      shawl,

I shall sing to you of an evening breeze
That rustles the palms where the hammocks swing
    in the jungle,
I shall tell of a sky full of stars,
Great stars, swollen big in their fullness of night.

In my guitar
You will hear fierce longings that have pulsed
    through Indian and Spaniard
For hundreds and hundreds of years,
Here, in these strings, the notes in their telling
Shall ripen and slip and fall
Like pear-shaped tears.

Listen!
Here is the laughter of naked brown maidens
Bathing at dawn in a mountain spring,
Here is the rustle of cornfields made fertile and
    green
By the labor of peons,
Here is the shine of dark eyes behind flowers
    and lace
At the vine-covered window
And the rhythmic upswing and downswing of yet-
    virgin hips
Under a dun earthen jar that is brimming with
    water,
The hot passion-turbulent moment, the flash of
    the blade,
The blood seeping
In my guitar.

Listen!
You are blonde, you are beautiful,

Cold arctic suns shine in you,
Let me darken you, warm you, envelop you whole
In the hot summer night of my love.

With my guitar
In a Tokyo bar.

—1946

Balada de la vida airada

Me voy a declarar en bancarrota,
tanto han mermado
todos los tesoros de mi juventud:
polvo de ilusiones, sueños disecados,
cáscaras de la varita de virtud
y uno que otro sapo almibarado.

Yo te los cedo, vida;
págate y págate, vieja malévola,
no me chupes ya la sangre
    y déjame empezar.

Antes
fueron mis dentros una flor de fuego
una llama hirviente que chisporroteaba,
y me chorreaban versos por los ojos,
por las orejas
y hasta por las narcies,
sí
    pero no.
La veta encendida ya se consumió
    y de las cenizas
    quedó una bola dura
    del tamaño de un frijol.

Un frijol arrugado que yace solitario en el vacío
    inmenso de todo mi interior.

Cuando me hieren, salta;
cuando me quieren, salta;
y si la luz lo toca
se baila un jarabe como avispa loca

pero sigue siendo
    un
      frijol.

Tómalo, vida, tómalo de rédito siquiera;
ten, vieja malévola,

    un frijol.

              —Tokio
               1946

Segunda ola

Llegando a la playa,
como quien dice en terreno ganado,
cuando de repente
¡ah, qué tronerilla de los condenados!
así adelantito iba Chicho el Urraco
y allí lo panciaron.

Y que se me prende la bota, hermano:
"¡Dame agua, cuñao! ¡dame agua, cuñao!"

¿Cómo l'iba a dar agua?
... allí agazapado ...
¡y no nos dejaban!

Pobrecito de Chicho, que le haiga tocado
llegando a la playa.

—1946

Gamagori

There's a girl in Gamagori
When it's spring
I will go to Gamagori
Where it lies beneath the shadow of the
    green and purple hills
When the plum has blossomed in the snow
I'll go
Then I'll go to Gamagori where it lies
    against the sand
Like a white and coral bather stretched
    asleep
In between the beer-foam breakers and
    the land
When the fishing boats are drawn in
    slender rows along the shore
And the wind comes singing softly as it
    used to do before
Then I'll go to Gamagori
In the spring
When the cherry buds awaken and the
    hill birds sing.

—Tokyo
1946

Ruégale a Dios

Ecos de violines húngaros
en las noches de Shanghai
y recuerdos de unos ojos
verdes como un limonar
en el mes de primavera.

Limoncito, limoncito,
la metralla del granizo
romper las puertas quisiera.[10]

—Shanghai
1946

Polaca de Tiensín

Polaca de Tiensín, tus ojos trágicos
me dejaron el fondo de negrura
de una noche sin fin:
música de Chopin y tu hermosura,
polaca de Tiensín.

Yo crucé por tu vida, pasajero,
insaciable viajador
entre el alba brillante de un "te quiero"
y el gris atardecer de un nuevo adiós.

Ahora nos separa un continente,
el avión se desliza
igual que tu música doliente
por la noche sin fin.
Sin el amancer de tu sonrisa,
polaca de Tiensín.

—1946

The Travelers

We are the lonely men,
We are the travelers.

We are the Capuchins
Of the hotel-room cloisters,
Prophets of bawdy words
And chaste remembrances,
We are the hermits of the moving throngs,
We are the travelers.

A glass of whisky is a trusted friend
And here and there a woman warms our bed
During the long, long winters,
We are the travelers.

—Changchun, Manchuria
December 24, 1946

Mukden Incident

The daughter of the mayor of Harbin
Is educated, elegant, and tiny,
Her face is pale as tea, her hair is shiny
With imported brilliantine;
She looks like a veritable queen
In her placid, unconcerned Oriental way.

(She doesn't think that dancing is a sin.)

The daughter of the mayor of Harbin
Is languishing in boredom after college in Fukien
And blames it on the foolishness of men.
She humbly begs my pardon:
The general has said we're going in
    To Harbin;
Then everything will be as it has been.

(She thinks I ought to learn some Mandarin.)

                                        —Mukden, Manchuria
                                        December 31, 1946

From a Traveler's Diary

Looking into a flower shop
I saw her face
reflected against the colors
that were behind the glass.

I turned and met her eyes
and for an instant there we both knew one another.

Then we passed each other by
and lost ourselves among the crowd.

March first, Shanghai.

—1947

Song in Red Flat

Red-painted, maggot-feverish
Whore of the East, Shanghai
You of the brilliant, stinking streets
Goodbye
I'm sorry to leave you, goodbye.

They say you are dying
I have touched your scabrous and puckered-up sores
Where even the pus has departed
You are a veteran whore dying of syphilis
Your face gaudily daubed
Your wasted-out body in costly and colorful plumage.

So I came to you and was kissed by you
What if between kisses
You bit my mouth, left it bleeding
Still you say to me:
Come out
Come to my alien streets
Into my moving and elbowing crowds
Fight your way through them, mix with them
Be part of them
And then you will know.

—1947

Caminata en La menor

Viajero, viajero
¿a dónde vas, compañero?
llevando en vilo
esa visión despiadada;
espera, espera
la mañana venidera
para seguirle de filo
a la quebrada.

No puedo, no puedo, hermana,
el horizonte distante
me llama,
con voces de brujería
reclama
mi ausencia la lejanía;
habré de seguir andante
hasta no ver muy del todo
las cortinas de una casa
aglobadas por el soplo
del levante.

—1947

Miné-ko

Let us remember Miné-ko

she was a vase
made of the finest of chinas

slender and pale
smooth to the touch
almost transparent

men came from faraway lands
and poured unto her
their love and their loneliness

that was Miné-ko

never had gonorrhea
incubated in such a receptacle.

—Tokyo
1947

Time Runs

Time
runs out of my hands like water
as I bring it to my lips
burning with thoughts of your secret fountains.

Let
me scoop the shimmering drops
as always beyond the reach
of all my hoping.

—1947

Diálogo de la vida vendida

Dizquepueta, public relations man
haciéndola de soldado,
metido en hotel de lujo
con una gringa a tu lado
(vamos a jugar
al hole-in-one
pues hay buena cancha para el torneo).

Aprendiz de brujo
del palabreo
¿cuántas camisas
son las que necesitas
habiendo tan buen jabón?
y ¿qué tal te queda la bata de seda?
(Ay, qué acedos, señor don Simón).

Ven otra vez y dime
que el poeta es pendejo sublime,
mas quedas perplejo
al pensar que se pasan los años,
eres nada sublime
(Pero sí más viejo).

Poco a poco te cercan los días
con vendaje de mierda enyesada
y todos tus sueños
y tus ambiciones
se mueren de tisis en las bartolinas
de la realidad
(Y todo es harina del mismo costal).

—Fujiyama
1947

Second Thoughts

We thought
"It must be love"
But it was not, in truth
Only a lonely summer's dream
And youth.

But then
Groping around
The outer edge of things
We woke to this world of cuckolds
And kings.

—Tokyo
1947

Hello Goodbye Hello

Through a looking glass, through a looking glass
Through a looking glass the colors are brighter
Through a looking glass
We see the faces that we think we love
Through a looking glass we think we see
Through a dream reflection
Through a lens, through a camera's eye
The colors are brighter in the city streets
And the motes are sunbeams.

Hello Ginza, goodbye Shanghai
And most of all
Jonesville-on-the Grande, goodbye.

Once I turned to you as a lover turns
I who last saw you six thousand miles ago
But I will now return
Through a looking glass I will return
I will come back again, turning as a lover turns
Full of sweet dreams and health and quiet whisky
Oh joy forever, full of tart desire.

                                          —1947

Gringa

Héla
diosa güera
bailando y cantando
va recogiendo las flores
muertas.

—1947

Korea

When the falling snow
Had covered the old plum tree
We dreamed of the spring,

Now I am alone
Under the falling blossoms
Of the sakura.

—

Because
Tears are such a waste
Pain comes a little harder
Than for most to you and me,
Ours is a smiling
And a frugal people.

—

The face
Of the Chōsen people
Is the face of a baby
That has lived ten thousand years,
That is why their flag
Is red and blue.

—Seoul
1948

Army of Occupation Types

The Shit-House Analyst

To prove a point
I'll tell you, see?

Two things, two things alone
Exist within this universe!
   Life!
   Death!
And LOVE is both of them.

What is greater than Sex, the Great Impeller?
Giver and receiver both
The cog and the wheel together
You reach into the cosmos
And what do you come up with?

A fistful of pubic hair.

The Writer

Pica pica pic, pica pica pic
The quick brown fox jumped over the lazy dogs
The quick brown fox one of these days
I am going to write and write and write
Like one goddamned writing fool
That doesn't know when to stop
And then I'll put myself down on paper
So everyone can see and say
Just look at the bastard
And some will say isn't he beautiful
And others will say, why the phoney, the
   dirty sonofabitch

But I won't care
As long as they all can see me
Can see me there and say
Just look at the bastard.

The Civil Service Girl

Full-teated, eagle-eyed and bold of butt
She picks her way through lines of office desks
And thickets of martinis
Over a trail of lace, perfume and used-up con-
     doms
And every skirted step is sentineled
By anxious, aging warriors
Your spoilers and your slaves
Callypygea.

—1948

Westward the Course of Empire

Favored by Rome's solicitude
Hannibal drank his potion
while Cuauhtémoc swung from a ceiba
without benefit of trial.

[handwritten: premier Tojo]
You, Hideki, had your day in court
people believe in being civilized
where we are from.

[handwritten: who is "we" and where are they from?]

[handwritten: mexican?]

Through the quickening twilight the bayonets
    gleam
the warheads are at ready
Carthage, city of triremes
Tenochtitlán, city of lakes
your time will come.[11]   *[handwritten: fallen empire]*

[handwritten: Amer. crimes will also bé ms put on trial.]

—Tokyo
December 24, 1948

[handwritten: Rise + fall of empires]

[handwritten: Empires super ceding Empires or Empires + Republics]

Song for a Flute of Clay

Mother I said you have forsaken me
This is for you my love
This cake of maize
And this
The little piping song
That I come singing
So harvesters may hear
This is for you
This little drop of blood.

Yet there are times
When one cares not to sing
Yes there are times
Oh bountiful
Such is the irony
Such is the agony
We bear
When burdened by the weight of day-by-day
We struggle trapped in darkness
Wishing a set of nerve ends burst in blood
Could be exchanged
For a belly full of health
Asking to be fed forever
Yes there are times oh Mother
There have been times.

And the harvesters harvest the grain
For the three-times daily bread that kills us
And the world moves on spins crazily by
A hard green shell with nothing inside
Burst at the seams like a second-hand boiler
And everyone looks

And nobody knows.

And so to sleep to eat to intercourse
And all the time the roving eye the ear
Attentive to the tread above our burrow
And nobody knows oh Mother nobody knows
Nobody knows but you who see us here
As we put away
The naked imbecility
To bed
Until another day.

—1949

Esquinita de mi pueblo

At the corner of absolute elsewhere
And absolute future I stood
Waiting for a green light
To leave the neighborhood

But the light was red
Forever and ever
The light was red
And all that tequila
Was going to my head.

That is the destiny of people in between
To stand on the corner
Waiting for the green.

—1950

Pito Pérez's Epitaph

And because it warmed my backside
I should thank the fuckin sun?
As a child I was a scholar,
As a man I was a bum,
As a married man, a cuckold,
Damned to hell when life is done.
Should I take it as a favor?
Should I thank the fuckin sun?[12]

—1950

Poems for Paleontologists

I

The Strongylocentrotus
Lives in the sea
He has his mouth
Where his arse should be
Centered quite neat
On his pants's seat
And how he knows
If he comes or goes
Is a mystery.
Let us avoid
The echinoid.

II

It was a pale Pelecypod
That never saw the sun
But spent his life contentedly
The ocean floor upon
He liked it well
Within his shell
He was his mother's son.

III

Then came a grasping Graptolite
That on the sea did sail
Who had not thought advisable
To have a coat of mail
Lament it might
This oversight
And all to no avail.

—1950

Deep Canyon

How long have we stood
Here on the brink
Looking away and down
Hoping to see
Timeless processions moving endlessly
Out of the stone
And thus to prove
That mountains move
And we are not alone.

The softer rock
Yields to the river's flow
To the dark current's lagging play
But there below
The jagged vomit of volcanic cysts
Bandaged in mist and spray
Thrusts forth its blackness like a waiting fear
That will not waste away.

—1951

El hijo

Aquí están las normas y las tradiciones
que trae en las venas el que habla español,
aquí están los sueños y las ilusiones
de un antiguo pueblo nacido del sol;

aquí van plasmadas las aspiraciones
que el tiempo impaciente no nos permitió
y también la ciencia de generaciones,
el ritmo de viejas y nuevas canciones
    y va nuestro Yo.

Un hijo es el centro del círculo trágico
que traza el destino, geómetra mágico
    del ser y no ser;
y es hondo misterio, antiguo, inmutable,
botón floreciente de carne palpable
    que espigó en la mujer.

—1951

All Together Now

Bevel the edges square
Plunge in the round round roundelay
The cessant pool that gives you style
And all the while
Avoiding sharpness darkness frown and fuss
Play not the fool be one of us
Be beautiful be fair
Bevel the edges square.

—1953

Claro de luna

Until I get
A plastic bubble for a head
And two tickets, reserved
On the Space Unlimited
The moon shall be the moon.

Where is it?
Said the little boy.
Is it the one the Russians made?

—1958

A Prayer for One's Forty-Fifth Birthday

πάτερ ἡμῶν
You of the Holy Writ,
Pity we beg of Thee
For we are all alone
Upon a boundless sea
   Of shit.
Not floating on the top
But all the way down
   In it.
Father all glorious,
O'er all victorious,
Be kind in killing us.
   Amen.

—1960

Midafternoon

The bolt is shot, the string has been unstrung,
   The song is ended.
This is the slack of time, the siesta sleep
When eyes are heavy and the slumbers light,
Light and uneasy for the bone's dull aching.

This is the way that it has always been
   So why the strangeness?
That it should happen here again, in this small
   space,
   Proud flicker of desire
That once burned fiercely and will soon expire.

—1966

From
Cantos a Carolina
1934 – 1946

I.

Ojos verdes, ojos verdes,
de suave mirar tan triste,
ojos que visten el alma
del color que el bosque viste.

Lagos verdes y profundos
con trazos de gris en ellos
do las nubes del cariño
reflejan sombra y destellos.

Ojos verdes, tristes, bellos,
tema de mi alabanza;
ojos color de follaje,
primavera y esperanza.

II.

Quién fuera rayo de blanca luna,
quién fuera lira con dulce voz,
quién fuera onda de la laguna:
    ¡quién fuera Dios!

Para bañarte con luz de plata,
para cantarte una serenata,
y acariciarte con mi agua azul:

¡para saber si me quieres tú!

III.

Luz del oro,
luz del mar,
luz de dulzura sin par.

Luz dorada de quimera
en tu rubia cabellera;
verde luz en tu mirada
como el mar en primavera.

Luz del oro,
luz del mar,
no te apartes de mí
jamás.

V.

Ojos mareños,
ojos de luz,
ojos risueños
de verde azul,

en tus pupilas
llenas de amor
bebió el cariño
que en mí nació.

Ojos tristes,
soñadores,
yo también soñé de amores.

Yo también.

VI.

Sé que habrás de marcharte,
tu destino lo exige,
pues tu sangre y mi sangre
no se deben mezclar;
nos separan los dejos
de una escuálida historia
y la inmunda memoria
de una saña mortal.

Sé que nunca en mis brazos
temblará tu cintura,
que es extraña locura
en tu cuerpo pensar;
sin embargo yo sueño
con la rara delicia
de gozar tus caricias
¿por qué no he de soñar?

IX.

Lágrimas que brotáis dentro del pecho
como brota la sangre en las entrañas
de una herida mortal,
subid, subid hasta que al fin me ahogue—
mis ojos no pueden más llorar.

Chispa veloz de loco pensamiento
cual rayo en tempestad,
traza su dulce imagen en la sombra—
mis ojos no la han de ver jámas.

XVI.

Cada vez que te sueño todavía
busca la soledad mi corazón
para gozar a solas la agonía
de tan íntimo dolor.

¿Cómo podrá mi corazón perderte
y mi mente dejar de recordarte?
Fuiste dulzura y luz;
no sé por qué sería yo tan ciego
o tan esquiva tú.

XXVI.

Coplero que cantó con su guitarra
sordos cantares que por fin se acaban,

   ¡Ah, guitarrero!

y si cruzaras el mundo entero
¿quién de tu nombre se acordará?
se fue la novia de la ventana,
no cantes más.

XXIX.

Dentro del silencio
que aborda la nada,
oculta en la sombra
de noche callada,
una voz se queja,
una voz se queja
en dolor sin fin.

Es la voz helada
del clarín que llora,
son sus notas pálidas
lágrimas del viento:
¡Silencio! ¡Silencio!
Duerme el campamento.
Y en la noche escueta
me acuerdo otra vez de ti.

XXX.

Fuente de mis más íntimas memorias,
amor de juventud, aún te sueño
en las noches de invierno,

y es dulce todavía tu recuerdo
con un dulzor que se convierte en pena
pues no han podido desmentir los años
la verdad de tu ausencia.

Epilogue

Canto de la muerte joven

—*a Rubén Salazar*
y a todos los demás

¿Y luego? ...
¿De allí a dónde? ...

   Después de decirle al mundo
que chingue su santa madre,
pues no tengo el pico chueco
ni hay perro que a mí me ladre ...

¿De allí a dónde? ...

   Después de que me desbuche
diciéndoles lo que siento,
lo que han hecho con nosotros
por tan largo, largo tiempo ...

¿Y luego? ...

   Después de todas la marchas
y toda la discusión,
los discursos, los disparos,
los comités en sesión ...

¿Y luego? ...
Carnales ...
¿De allí a dónde? ... [13]

—1970

Notes and Random Comments

[1]Published in the (Harlingen) *Valley Morning Star*, October 1934. The *Star* printed several others of my compositions. Odd in retrospect, since Harlingen at the time was extremely racist.

[2]Perhaps the best known of my efforts at versifying. The first version was done in Spring 1934, when I was a senior in high school. Composed while walking the 21 blocks home from school one afternoon and written down—with revisions—shortly afterward. This second, written version became current in manuscript form in south Texas, was used in political campaigns, was reprinted a few times as anonymous, and entered oral tradition locally. Collected in Brownsville as "folk poetry" in the 1960s by a student of one of my colleagues, Roger D. Abrahams. When it began to circulate in manuscript, writer Hart Stilwell criticized the language as sounding too much like the stage "Italian" dialect of the time. I made revisions and it is this third version, done in 1935, that appears here.

[3]First published in the *Southwest Review* (Autumn 1964).

[4]Written on occasion of the Texas Centennial celebrations. *La Prensa* of San Antonio, then an outlet for some of my verse in Spanish, declined to print it.

[5]First published in *El Regional* (Matamoros, Tamaulipas) in 1938.

[6]On January 6, 1941, President Roosevelt enunciated his principle of the "Four Freedoms" that should prevail throughout the world once the Axis powers were defeated. Included were "freedom from want" (rich nations would help poor nations rather than exploit them) and "freedom from fear" (powerful nations would not commit acts of physical aggression against weaker ones). Some people were skeptical.

[7]Parodies some lines by local poets.

[8]I no longer remember when or where I discovered Adelaide Crapsey and her "cinquains," but I liked the form and used it a number of times in both English and Spanish. The syllabic verse and the stanza pattern (2/4/6/8/2) remind one of Hispanic poetry in the *arte menor* tradition. Some other cinquains are included in this volume.

[9]The title alludes to a song in oral tradition for several generations before World War II. It began, "La tarde era triste, la nieve caía." Or as one local character, serving with the AEF during World War I, translated it, "The evening was sad, the ice cream was falling."

[10]The title alludes to a *son* dating at least to the turn of the century: "Limoncito, limoncito/ si no quieres que te quiera/ limoncito, limoncito/ ruégale a Dios que me muera." The *son* gained bicultural exposure as part of the repertoire of Luisa Espinel, who toured the U.S. with a program of Southwest Mexican songs in the mid-1930s, which she called "Songs My Mother Taught Me." She was popular enough to be parodied in a booklet called "Songs My Mother Never Taught Me." If I am not mistaken, Luisa Espinel is or was related to Linda Rondstat, who has produced a show of her own called "Songs My Father Taught Me."

[11]Hideki Tojo and his fellow "war criminals" were hanged on December 23, 1948, earlier than scheduled, we were told, so that our Christmas holidays would not be spoiled.

[12]Rendering of a passage from José Rubén Romero's picaresque novel, *La vida inútil de Pito Pérez*.

[13]On March 29, 1970, TV journalist Rubén Salazar died after being struck on the head by a tear-gas projectile fired by a member of the Los Angeles police department, as Salazar drank a beer in an L.A. bar. A Chicano demonstration was taking place nearby. The police officers responsible

were later acquitted of violating Salazar's civil rights. Rudy Acuña's *Occupied America* has an account of the incident.